Protecting Habitats

Oceans in Danger

Anita Ganeri

W
FRANKLIN WATTS
LONDON•SYDNEY

Designer Rita Storey
Editor Sarah Ridley
Art Director Jonathan Hair
Editor-in-Chief John C. Miles
Picture Research Susan Mennell
Map artwork Ian Thompson

© 2004 Franklin Watts

First published in 2004
by Franklin Watts
96 Leonard Street
London
EC2A 4XD

Franklin Watts Australia
45-51 Huntley Street
Alexandria
NSW 2015

ISBN 0 7496 5818 5

A CIP catalogue record for this book is
available from the British Library.

Printed in Hong Kong/China

Picture Credits
Cover images: Ecoscene (left and centre);
Still Pictures (right)

Ecoscene: pp.1, 9, 13, 14, 15, 19, 20, 21, 22
Science Photo Library: p.11
Still Pictures: pp.5, 6, 7, 16, 17, 18, 23, 24,
26-27

Every attempt has been made to clear copyright.
Should there be any inadvertent omission, please
apply to the publisher for rectification.

Note to parents and teachers
Every effort has been made by the Publishers to ensure that the
websites in this book are suitable for children, that they are of the
highest educational value, and that they contain no
inappropriate or offensive material. However, because of the
nature of the Internet, it is impossible to guarantee that the
contents of these sites will not be altered. We strongly advise that
Internet access is supervised by a responsible adult.

CONTENTS

What are the oceans?

From space, our planet Earth looks blue because over two-thirds of it is covered in seawater. This lies in five oceans which, together, contain a staggering 97% of all the world's water. The oceans merge to form a vast, continuous expanse of sea, and the largest environment for living things on Earth.

The five oceans

In order of size, the five oceans are the Pacific, Atlantic, Indian, Southern and Arctic. The Pacific is the largest ocean by far, covering one-third of the Earth and stretching, at its widest point, almost halfway around the world. It also has the deepest water, with an average depth of about 4 km (2.5 miles). It plunges to 11 km (6.8 miles) at its deepest point, in the Marianas Trench. About one-tenth of the size of the Pacific, the Arctic is the smallest of the world's

oceans. It is also the shallowest, with an average depth of 1.3 km (0.8 miles). For most of the year, the Arctic Ocean is covered in a layer of floating ice, up to 3 m (10 ft) thick.

The origins of oceans

Planet Earth was formed about 4,600 million years ago, from a cloud of swirling gases and dust. The great heat produced as the Earth formed meant that the new planet consisted of molten (melted) rock. As it cooled and solidified, a thin, rocky crust was made. Many volcanoes covered the Earth's surface at this time, releasing vast quantities of water vapour into the atmosphere. As the Earth cooled further, this water vapour condensed to create storm clouds and rain. Gradually, low-lying areas filled with water to form the first oceans, which scientists think date from 3,800 million years ago.

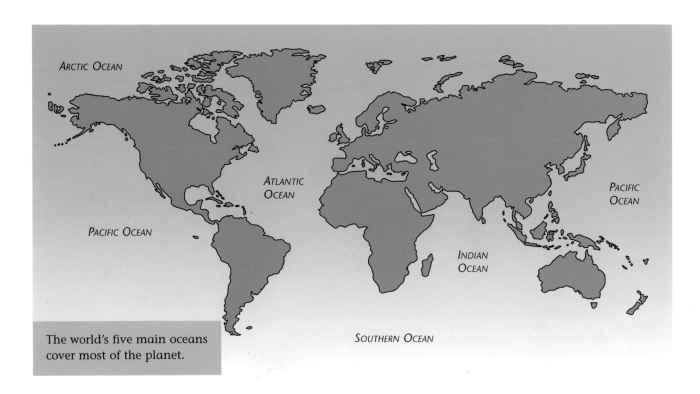

The world's five main oceans cover most of the planet.

UNDER THREAT

Today, the Earth's oceans are under serious threat. Overfishing, illegal fishing and marine pollution are just some of the major problems affecting seas all over the world. They are destroying this fragile habitat and putting its wildlife and people in grave danger. Scientists are working hard to learn more about the sea and about how to manage ocean resources better. This book looks at some of the problems facing the oceans, and at the measures being taken to study them and protect them for the future.

Salty seawater

A key feature of seawater is its saltiness (called salinity). Seawater is salty because it contains large amounts of sodium chloride, or common salt. Most of this salt comes from rocks on land and is washed into the sea by rivers. Some comes from volcanoes under the sea.

Salinity is measured as the number of grams of salt dissolved in one kilogram (2.2 lb) of water. On average, a litre of seawater contains about 35 g (1 oz) of salt, though salinity varies from place to place. It can be lower in places where fresh water enters the sea from melting icebergs, glaciers and rainfall. It can be higher in warm places, where the heat causes fresh water to evaporate, leaving a higher concentration of salt behind.

Under threat: a school of brightly coloured fish swim past a coral formation in the Red Sea.

Under the sea

The oceans fill enormous, bowl-shaped dips, known as basins. But the floor of these ocean basins is not flat and featureless. There are gigantic mountain ranges, towering volcanoes, plunging valleys and vast plains, just as there are on dry land.

Edges of continents

Around the edges of the continents, the land slopes from the coast into the deep sea. Known as continental margins, these areas include the continental shelf, slope and rise, which vary in width, depth and steepness around the different continents. The continental shelf slopes gently out to sea, up to about 60 km (37 miles) from the shoreline. At the edge of the shelf, the seabed falls away steeply. This is the continental slope, which reaches a depth of about 3 km (2 miles). Sediment flows down the slope, forming a thick layer at the bottom, called the continental rise. It slopes more gently to the seabed.

At a depth of about 4 to 6 km (2.5 to 3.5 miles), the continental margin ends and the abyssal plains begin. These vast, usually flat plains cover over half of the ocean floor. They are carpeted in a thick layer of sediment. This is formed from the bodies of billions of tiny plants and animals, as well as mud, sand and silt washed into the sea by rivers.

Sea-floor features

The Earth's rocky, outer crust is split into seven huge, and many smaller, pieces called tectonic plates. The plates float like giant rafts on the semi-molten rocks beneath. As they collide or drift apart, they create dramatic seabed features and change the size and shape of the ocean basins.

Many sea animals make their homes on continental margins. Here, different forms of marine life inhabit a shipwreck.

DISCOVERING SEAMOUNTS

Seamounts are huge, extinct volcanoes which tower up from the seabed. There are as many as 30,000 seamounts scattered throughout the oceans. Until recently, little was known about life around seamounts. Now, using deep-sea video cameras, scientists are finding out more about these unique habitats. They have discovered hundreds of animal species which are new to science. Among them are sponges, sea fans and small fish which feed from the nutrient-rich currents flowing around the seamounts.

Huge waves crash against a seamount, photographed off the coast of South America.

Where two plates pull apart under water, molten rock from deep beneath the Earth rises to fill the gap. As it solidifies, it forms a new ocean crust and pushes the older crust away on either side. This is called sea-floor spreading. Over millions of years, the new crust builds huge mountain ranges known as spreading ridges. The longest is the Mid-Atlantic Ridge, in the Atlantic Ocean.

Even though new ocean crust is constantly being made, the Earth is not getting bigger. Where two plates collide underwater or at the edge of a continent, one plate is pushed downwards and melts back into the Earth. This is called subduction and it balances out the effect of sea-floor spreading. Subduction creates long, narrow valleys, called trenches, in the sea floor.

Why are oceans important?

The oceans are vitally important to our world. Millions of years ago, the earliest life on Earth began in the sea. Today, tiny ocean plants, called phytoplankton, produce half of the oxygen we breathe through photosynthesis. They also soak up vast quantities of carbon dioxide which would otherwise add to global warming (see p 21).

The oceans are home to millions of plants and animals, and form the largest habitat on Earth. They also play a major part in the world's weather and climate. Ocean resources – such as oil and fish – heat our homes, run our cars and fill our stomachs.

Climate control

The oceans are vital in regulating the world's climate. Seawater is constantly moving. The wind drives huge bands of water, called surface currents, which flow around the world. These currents may be as warm as 30°C (86°F) or as cold as –2°C (27°F). They have a great effect on the world's climate. In the tropics, the currents soak up the Sun's heat. They carry this heat to colder regions, then gradually release it. This spreads heat more evenly around the world. Without these ocean currents, the poles would get colder and colder, and the tropics unbearably hot.

Currents also affect the climate of the land masses they pass by. The Gulf Stream transports warm water from the Caribbean along the east coast of North America, then across the Atlantic Ocean to Europe. The enormous amount of heat it carries helps to make the climate of north-west Europe much milder than that of places on the same latitude on the other side of the ocean.

Ocean resources

From the oxygen we breathe to the fish we eat, the oceans are extremely rich in natural resources. Each year, about 75 million tonnes of fish are taken from the sea. Much of this is caught by modern, commercial fleets, equipped with the latest technology for locating fish shoals. About one-fifth of the oil and natural gas we use comes from under the sea. The oceans also provide transport routes, sources of renewable energy, such as tidal power, and are popular places for leisure activities. Unfortunately, exploitation of these resources is leading to problems for the oceans and damaging these fragile habitats.

THE WATER CYCLE

The Earth's water supply is constantly recycled in the water cycle. The oceans play a crucial part in this process: the Sun's heat causes millions of litres of water to evaporate from the Earth's surface. It comes from the soil, lakes, rivers and the oceans, and rises into the air as water vapour. As the air rises and cools, the water vapour condenses into tiny droplets. These join to form clouds which release water as rain or snow. Some water falls in the oceans, lakes and rivers. Some soaks into the soil. Then the water cycle begins again.

Extracting oil and gas from the seabed involves
the construction of pipelines and huge production
platforms, such as this one in the North Sea.

The web of life

The oceans form the largest habitat on Earth. They are home to a huge variety of living things, from tiny plants to enormous whales. Animals live in every part of the sea, from the surface water to the seabed.

Zones of life

Different parts of the sea vary in depth, the amount of light they receive and in water temperature. This affects the type of animal living there. Scientists divide the sea into different zones of life, based on depth. The epipelagic zone reaches from the surface down to about 100 to 150 m (330 to 490 ft). Its most important feature is that it is lit by the Sun, allowing plants to photosynthesize. Below this is the mesopelagic zone, also called the twilight zone. Its upper part is still light, but below about 1,000 m (3,200 ft), the water is permanently dark because the Sun's light cannot reach this far. The third zone, called the abyssal zone, receives no sunlight at all. Here the water is always pitch black and freezing cold.

The seabed is called the benthic zone and the animals that live here are known as the benthos. Many of them lie buried in the sediment, hidden from view. Until about 100 years ago, scientists did not believe that anything could live below a depth of a few hundred metres. Modern technology, such as submersibles (see p 25), has shown that benthic animals are found even at depths of over 10 km (6 miles).

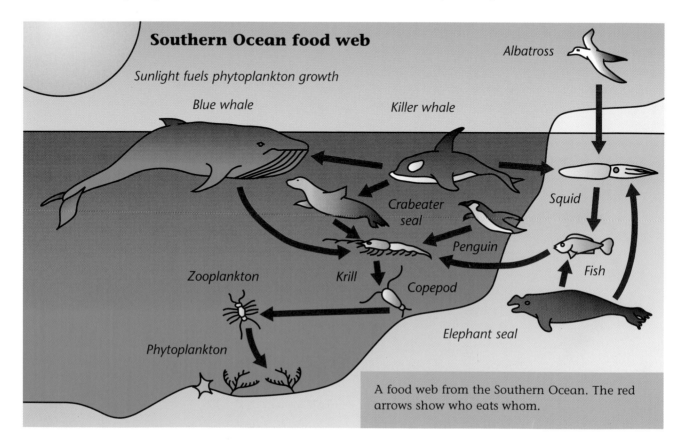

Southern Ocean food web

Sunlight fuels phytoplankton growth

Albatross

Blue whale

Killer whale

Crabeater seal

Squid

Penguin

Fish

Zooplankton

Krill

Copepod

Phytoplankton

Elephant seal

A food web from the Southern Ocean. The red arrows show who eats whom.

A magnified view of marine phytoplankton. The entire ocean food web starts with this.

Plants for food

As on land, ocean plants and animals are linked together by what they eat. Every ocean food chain begins with microscopic, single-celled plants, called phytoplankton. These are essential to life in the oceans because they make their own food, grow and multiply by photosynthesis. In turn, they are grazed by tiny animals, called zooplankton, which provide food for many larger animals.

Because plants need sunlight to make food, phytoplankton are only found in the upper 150 to 200 m (490 to 650 ft) of the sea. About 20,000 million tonnes of phytoplankton grow each year. The amount varies from place to place, being especially rich over the continental shelves. Here the water contains plenty of nutrients, which the plants need to grow. In turn, the plants are food for large numbers of fish – this is where most of the world's catch comes from.

Plant growth is also affected by the time of year. In winter, in temperate oceans, storms whip up the water, stirring up the nutrients that rise to the surface. In spring, phytoplankton take advantage of this nutrient supply – and the longer hours of sunlight – to form enormous "blooms". These offer plenty of food for fish which, in turn, make rich pickings for seabirds and whales. By late summer, the nutrient supply runs out and the phytoplankton die back.

The blooms colour the water cloudy green. The greener the water, the more phytoplankton it contains. Scientists are developing satellites to detect slight changes in sea colour which signify various types and quantities of phytoplankton. This will allow scientists to monitor the blooms, and the overall health of the oceans.

On the edge

For plants and animals living on coasts, daily life is a struggle to survive. Every day, the shore is battered by waves, and the tides rise and fall. These plants and animals must cope with being covered in water, then left high and dry. They have many special features to help them stay alive.

Battered by waves

The shape of the world's coastlines is constantly changing as waves pound against the shore. Waves are caused by the action of the wind blowing across the surface of the sea. Stones and pebbles carried by the waves grind away at rocky coasts, wearing them away. Along some coasts, this creates dramatic features, such as arches, sea stacks and sheer cliffs, which provide nesting sites for colonies of seabirds.

Turning tides

Twice a day, the sea rises and floods the shore at high tide. Then it falls, or ebbs, away at low tide. The tides are mainly caused by the pull of the Moon and Sun's gravity on the oceans. This pull causes the water nearest the Moon to form a gigantic bulge. To balance this out, the Earth's spin pulls the oceans on the opposite side into another bulge.

The tidal range is the difference between the height of sea level at high and low tide. This is affected by the shape of the nearby land. Along open coasts, the tidal range is usually between 2 to 3 m (6 to 10 ft). In almost land-locked seas, such as the Mediterranean, the range is less than 1 m (3 ft). The greatest difference is in the Bay of Fundy, in south-eastern Canada, which has a tidal range of over 15 m (50 ft).

Staying alive

The intertidal zone is a tough place to live, for conditions are always changing. When the tide goes out, animals are left exposed and run the risk of drying out. Many filter food from the water so, at low tide, they can no longer feed.

Animals have evolved various methods of protection against these threats. Limpets and barnacles seal themselves in their shells and cling onto rocks. Crabs hide in damp cracks in rocks or in rock pools, while lugworms burrow in the sand.

Another danger for living things is being swept out to sea. Mussels hold on to

TURTLES UNDER THREAT

All over the world, coastal regions and their wildlife are under threat from pollution and the development of tourist beaches and hotels. Sea turtles use sandy shores as nesting sites. But threats, such as habitat destruction and hunting for meat, eggs and shells, are wiping out thousands of turtles a year. Today, out of the seven turtle species, three are facing extinction, three are endangered and the seventh is very rare.

rocks with a "beard" of strong fibres, made by glands in their bodies. Fish, such as gobies, have specially adapted pelvic (rear) fins that act as suction cups. Seaweeds have strong, root-like holdfasts to anchor themselves to the rocks.

A sea turtle digs a pit on a sandy beach in which to lay her eggs. All species of sea turtle worldwide are now endangered.

Coral reefs

Coral reefs are the richest and most varied habitats in the sea. They are sometimes compared to tropical rainforests on land. But all over the world, reefs are under threat from pollution and other human activities.

Reef-building coral

Coral reefs are built by tiny sea animals, called coral polyps, which are related to jellyfish and sea anemones. Their bodies contain millions of yellow-brown granules. These are tiny plants, called algae. The polyps and algae live in partnership. Through photosynthesis, the algae provide the polyps with food and oxygen. In return, the algae take in the polyps' waste products and have a safe home to live in.

Coral polyps live in huge colonies, many millions strong. The polyps build hard, stony cases around their soft bodies, using limestone, or calcium carbonate, from the water. Each species of coral builds its protective case in a different way, resulting in an amazing variety of shapes and patterns of coral. Most of the reef is made up of cases left behind when the polyps inside die. These build up in layers, with a thin layer of living corals on top.

Life on the reef

A coral reef is home to an astonishing range of fish and invertebrates, such as starfish, sea slugs, giant clams and octopus. Parrot fish feed directly on the corals, nipping off pieces with their sharp, beak-like teeth.

Corals can only live in warm, shallow, tropical seas because the algae inside them need sunlight to photosynthesize.

STARFISH DANGER

The Great Barrier Reef stretches for about 2,300 km (1,420 miles) along the northeast coast of Australia. Covering some 345,000 sq km (133,000 sq miles), it is the world's largest reef system. In the 1980s, large areas of coral reef were eaten away by millions of crown-of-thorns starfish. Scientists feared that the whole reef might be destroyed. Fortunately, the starfish numbers eventually grew less, leaving the reef to recover. It is thought that these swarms may happen when shell-collectors upset the balance by taking too many giant triton shells, which themselves eat the starfish.

A crown-of-thorns starfish feeds on coral.

Clams and barnacles bore holes in the coral reef to hide in while they filter food from the water. Groupers are large fish which lurk in small caves, hardly moving. When a smaller fish comes close, the grouper suddenly strikes and seizes its prey.

Because the reef is so crowded, competition for food and space is fierce. Animals defend their territories ferociously to keep intruders away. Reef life is finely balanced between day- and night-time feeders. At daybreak, large numbers of fish leave their caves and holes to search for food. At sunset, they return to their hiding places and the nocturnal fish and invertebrates swarm out. Some fish, such as soldierfish, have very large eyes to help them find their prey in the dark.

Crowding is also the reason why many reef fish are so colourful. It is vital for individual fish to be able to find members of their own species so that they can pick out possible rivals and mates. The bright colours and striking patterns of reef fish, such as butterfly fish, act like identity tags so that the fish can recognize each other.

The open ocean

The streamlined blue marlin is one of the open ocean's greatest hunters.

The open ocean, or pelagic zone, stretches for thousands of kilometres beyond the continental shelves. It covers about 70% of the Earth's surface. This huge habitat is home to some amazing animals, many of which are designed for travelling vast distances in search of food or mates.

Ocean hunters

The open ocean is home to some of the sea's fastest and fiercest hunters, such as sharks, tuna and marlin. They have to cover vast areas in search of prey. To do this as efficiently as possible, their bodies are designed as swimming machines. The blue marlin, for example, has a streamlined body shape for cutting through the water, an upright dorsal (upper) fin for stabilizing its body as it swims, and crescent-shaped tail fins for propelling it along at maximum speed. Its spear-like "bill" can be used for hunting, self-defence and cutting through the water.

The sailfish is a superbly streamlined swimmer which hunts in the surface layer of tropical oceans. Over short distances, it is probably the fastest fish in the sea. It reaches speeds of over 130 km/h (80 mp/h) when chasing down its prey of fish and squid. Tuna are also thought to reach similar speeds.

Fish off the coast of Malaysia. Many species of fish group together in shoals for protection.

Shoals of fish

In the open ocean, there is nowhere to hide from enemies. So prey animals have developed a wide range of self-defence techniques. Herring are small fish, eaten by many ocean predators, such as dolphins and killer whales. They swim in enormous shoals of hundreds, or even thousands, of fish. At the first sign of danger, the herring form a huge, swirling ball. This helps to confuse predators and makes it harder for individual fish to be caught.

Vertical migration

Some prey animals try to avoid predators by waiting until it is dark to come to the surface to feed. Scientists are still finding out more about this process, which they call "vertical migration". Every night, at around dusk, millions of animals move upwards from the twilight zone of the ocean to the surface in search of food. At daybreak, they swim back down again and spend the day out of sight of predators. The length of these migrations varies according to the animals' size. Tiny animals, like zooplankton, migrate only 10 to 20 m (30 to 60 ft). Larger sea animals may travel 1,000 m (3,000 ft) or more.

SHARK TAGGING

At up to 18 m (60 ft) long, whale sharks are the biggest fish in the sea. They feed on zooplankton which they sieve from the water. To locate the richest food supplies, whale sharks travel huge distances. Scientists are using satellite tags to track the sharks' movements. The sharks are fitted with electronic tags which transmit information to a satellite, then to a computer on land. A whale shark tagged in the Indian Ocean was found to travel almost 3,000 km (1,800 miles) in just ten days. Whale sharks are under threat from fishing and the information collected from the tags is being used to plan a conservation programme.

In the deep

The deeper you descend in the oceans, the colder and darker the water becomes. Below about 600 m (1,900 ft), there is no light at all. The pressure of the water is crushing. Yet, despite the harsh conditions, an astonishing number of animals live in the ocean depths.

Finding food

One of the main problems facing deep-sea creatures is finding food. Most deep-sea animals have adapted to take advantage of whatever food they can find. Gulper eels, for example, are found at depths of 2 km (1.2 miles) or below. Their bodies are made up mostly of huge, gaping mouths and large, stretchy stomachs, allowing them to swallow prey much larger than themselves. They hang in the water. Then, when their prey comes close enough, they open their gigantic mouths and gulp it down.

Most of the food that reaches the deep sea consists of the dead bodies of plants and animals that fall from the surface above. But food takes a very long time to sink the 5 to 10 km (3 to 6 miles) to the deep-sea floor. Scientists estimate that it takes a small dead shrimp about a week to fall just 3 m (9 ft). Much of this food is eaten or rots away on the way down.

Not a pretty sight: the deep-sea angler fish trails a lure above its mouth to attract prey.

Light in the darkness

Many deep-sea animals produce their own biological light, called bioluminescence. Some creatures make light by chemical reactions inside light-producing organs, called photophores, in their bodies. Others use bacteria living in their bodies to produce light for them. These lights have a number of functions. They may be used to confuse predators and to send signals to members of the same species, or to lure prey. The deep-sea angler fish has a long fin growing in front of its mouth, like a fishing rod. At the end is a glowing blob of light which acts like bait to tempt prey within range of the angler fish's huge mouth.

HYDROTHERMAL VENTS

In the late 1970s, deep-sea scientists investigating the Pacific Ocean discovered springs of hot water, called hydrothermal vents, gushing up from cracks in the seabed. The vents are home to huge colonies of animals, including tube worms 3 m (9 ft) long. Amazingly, the animals have their own unique food supply. The worms feed on bacteria living inside their bodies. In turn, the bacteria make food using minerals dissolved in the hot water. Most food chains begin with plants which use sunlight to make food. This is one of the few habitats on Earth which does not rely on the Sun's energy to survive.

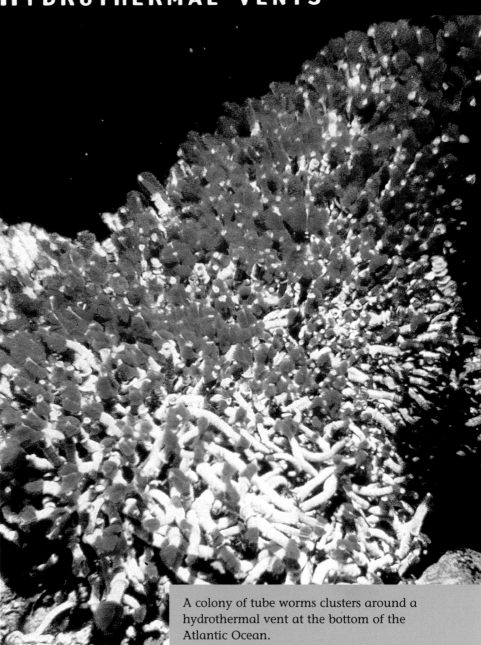

A colony of tube worms clusters around a hydrothermal vent at the bottom of the Atlantic Ocean.

Life on the deep-sea floor

The amazing creatures of the deep-sea floor range from single-celled animals to worms, shrimps, starfish and fish. Some are tiny and live buried in the sediment. Others, like sea cucumbers, crawl slowly across the sea floor, sucking up scraps to eat. Behind them, they leave criss-crossing tracks in the sediment.

The deep-sea tripod fish gets its name from its three extra-long fins. They extend underneath its body, like a camera tripod. The fish uses these to stand on the seabed while it waits for the current to bring it some food. Deep-sea fish are mainly black, dark-grey or brown – this provides them with camouflage in the murky darkness of the deep-sea water.

19

Oceans under threat

The world's oceans are under tremendous pressure. Environmental threats, such as marine pollution, drilling for oil and gas, global warming and overfishing are damaging these fragile habitats and putting the oceans under threat.

Marine pollution

For years, the oceans have been used as the largest rubbish tip on Earth. People thought that their sheer size could deal with whatever was dumped into them. Today, marine pollution is a serious problem. Huge amounts of industrial waste, sewage sludge, oil and plastics are disposed of at sea every year. Most of this pollution comes from land and is washed into the sea by rivers. Much of the rest is dumped from ships or pumped directly into the sea. Sometimes oil tankers run aground and spill thousands of tonnes of oil. Wherever it comes from, pollution damages the oceans, killing plants and animals and harming people who rely on the sea for food.

In some places, where sewage or fertilizers wash into the sea, the water becomes covered in a thick, reddish-brown slime. This is known as a "red tide". It is caused by a rapid growth of red algae, which feed on nutrients in the sewage. The algae block out sunlight and starve the water of oxygen so that fish and other animals suffocate.

Rescue workers struggled to save oil-soaked wildlife after a tanker, the *Prestige*, ran aground off the coast of Spain in 2002 and spilled its cargo.

EXTRACTING OIL AND GAS

About one-fifth of the world's oil and gas comes from under the sea. Since 1947, when the first offshore oil rig was set up in the Gulf of Mexico, oil and gas exploration has become big business. By the mid-1990s, there were almost 6,500 oil and gas platforms. Most are found on the continental shelves. But, with the growing demand for oil and gas, it seems likely that companies will want to drill in deeper and deeper waters. Environmentalists are concerned about the effects of this drilling on the fragile and unique deep-ocean habitat.

Global warming

Many scientists believe that the Earth is getting warmer because of the "greenhouse effect". Small amounts of CO_2 (carbon dioxide) and other "greenhouse" gases are found naturally in the atmosphere. Like the glass in a greenhouse, they help trap the Sun's heat, keeping the Earth warm enough for life to survive. But burning fossil fuels, such as oil and gas, is increasing the amount of CO_2. This is trapping too much heat and making the Earth too warm. This warming may also be partly due to natural climate change. By the year 2100, the Earth's temperature may have risen by about 2°C (4°F). This could melt the ice at the poles, raising sea levels by some 50 m (160 ft) and drowning low-lying coastal areas and islands around the world.

Scientists are also worried that the extra CO_2 is reacting with seawater and making the oceans too acidic. This process is happening too quickly for the oceans to adjust naturally. Experts are not yet sure what effect this might have on ocean wildlife. But they think that corals may be at greatest risk because the acid could dissolve the calcium carbonate that corals use to make their protective cases.

Seabirds and other creatures living on coasts are very vulnerable to oil spills.

Coral reefs at risk

All over the world, coral reefs are at risk. One-quarter of the world's reefs has already been destroyed. Another 60% are seriously threatened by human activities, such as pollution, mining for sand and rock, and harvesting of rare corals and shells. Fishing boats also smash and destroy reefs.

Another major threat to coral reefs is coral bleaching. Much of the corals' colour comes from the algae living inside the polyps. When the sea gets warmer, the algae die or the corals themselves push them out. Before long, the whole reef turns ghostly white. Coral bleaching may be the result of disease, lack of sunlight or a change in salinity. But the most likely cause is global warming (see p 21). If the water cools, the corals may recover. But if all the algae are lost, the corals will die and the reefs crumble. Scientists estimate that by the end of the 21st century coral bleaching will have killed half of the world's remaining reefs.

Coral reef destruction has a devastating effect on wildlife. But it is not only wildife at risk. In many poorer parts of the world, millions of people along the coast rely on coral reefs for their food, building materials and livelihoods. In Asia alone, coral reefs are home to about one-quarter of all the fish caught. Millions of tourists visit reefs each year to dive or snorkel, and this provides local people with much-needed income. The reefs also play a valuable part in protecting the shoreline from storm surges and erosion. Losing the reefs could spell disaster for these coastal communities.

Coral reefs – surrounding islands such as this one – are threatened in many different ways.

Overfishing

For centuries, people have relied on the sea for food. Millions of tonnes of fish and shellfish are caught every year. Many modern commercial fishing boats are equipped with computers, satellites and radar for locating fish, allowing them to catch more fish than ever. Today, overfishing is a serious problem and is upsetting the natural balance of the ocean habitat. So many fish are being caught that there is not time for the fish to breed, grow and for stocks to recover again. Many of the world's fisheries are overfished or on the edge of collapse. Fish that we once took for granted, such as cod, tuna and salmon, are no longer common. Between the years 2001 and 2002, the total weight of cod in the North Sea, for example, plummeted from 51,000 tonnes to 38,000 tonnes. If this continues, cod will die out for good.

DOLPHIN-FRIENDLY TUNA

Thousands of sea animals, like the dolphin shown below, are killed when they accidentally get caught up in fishing gear. They are known as by-catch. Tuna are one of the world's most valuable and popular types of fish. They often swim with large schools of dolphins, following them to find food. By chasing the dolphins, fishing boats were led to the tuna, then a net was set around the whole lot. Following an outcry in the 1980s, this form of fishing was banned and the number of dolphin deaths greatly reduced. Unfortunately, many other animals, such as sharks, have become by-catch instead.

What's being done?

Exploring the deeps: a ship-board scientist operates the controls of an ROV (remotely operated vehicle) on a research mission.

Around the world, scientists, conservation groups and governments are working hard to understand the oceans better in order to protect them and their unique wildlife. The oceans form such a vast habitat that, despite modern technology, we still know very little about them. Faced with the growing threat to the oceans, it is vital to find out more.

Exploring the oceans

Until about 50 years ago, scientists had very little idea about what lay beneath the sea. Today, there is still a vast amount of ocean to be explored but scientists have developed cutting-edge technology which allows them to investigate deeper than ever before.

Sound travels quickly through water. This is why ocean scientists often use sonar to map the deep-sea floor. Sonar instruments work by giving out sharp "bleeps" of sound. These hit parts of the seabed and send back echoes. From the pattern of the echoes, scientists can build up a picture of the sea floor, including features such as seamounts and trenches.

Scientists also use sound to keep in contact with instruments deep in the ocean. These instruments respond to sound signals sent to them by ships many kilometres away. Some are left in place on the seabed for over a year to collect samples or take measurements. They are attached to long wires, weighted down on the seabed, and fixed to air-filled floats. When they receive a sound signal, the wires are released from the weights. The floats bring the instruments to the surface where they are picked up by the research ship.

Deep-sea submersibles

A submersible is an underwater vehicle, like a miniature submarine, used to explore the deep sea. Some submersibles are unmanned robots or ROVs (remotely operated vehicles), which carry cameras and other sampling and measuring equipment. Some are attached to a research ship by a cable, along which information and instructions are sent. Free-swimming submersibles are also being developed. They will carry their own power supply and send data back to land through satellite links.

There are also manned submersibles which can carry scientists deep beneath the sea. The *Johnson Sealink II* is a modern, manned submersible, launched in Florida, USA. It can carry a crew of four and operate at depths of up to 3 km (1.8 miles). The submersible is equipped with a range of instruments, including suction devices and plankton samplers. It also has sonar, and both still and video cameras. To see in the dark water, it uses powerful arc lights which can create almost daylight conditions.

Satellite surveys

Satellites high above the Earth also observe the oceans. They have revolutionized ocean science because they can gather information much more quickly than research ships. Among other things, the data collected has allowed scientists to make detailed maps showing sea surface temperature, the patterns of ocean currents, and to monitor changes in sea level and the size and location of phytoplankton blooms.

A new satellite, *Aqua*, was launched by the USA in 2002. It is being used to study cloud features, phytoplankton and to collect information about the water cycle. From this, scientists are hoping to learn more about the connection between the oceans and climate change.

Saving the seas

Conservation groups, such as Greenpeace, the WWF (Worldwide Fund for Nature) and Conservation International are working hard to save the oceans from further harm. Since the 1980s, Greenpeace has been campaigning to stop the dumping of oil and gas rigs and radioactive waste in the sea. The WWF's "Endangered Seas" campaign is aimed at protecting marine habitats by reducing pollution, stopping the illegal trade in ocean wildlife and ending destructive fishing methods. The WWF works with governments around the world to help find ways for people to use the oceans without causing lasting harm. It also wants to see the introduction of more Fishing-Free Zones. These are areas closed to fishing where fish stocks can recover.

In April 2004, the WWF and Greenpeace won an important victory in their campaign to protect the Baltic Sea. The IMO (International Maritime Organization) decided to mark the sea as a "Particularly Sensitive Sea Area". The Baltic is one of the

world's busiest seas and oil spills from ship accidents were threatening the sea and its wildlife, particularly fish and migrating birds. The new measures mean that ships must take extra care, reducing the risk of accidents.

Protected areas

One way of saving the oceans may be to set aside certain areas as protected parks. These would safeguard endangered species and fish stocks, at the same time as making sure that local people can still earn a living. At present, only about 0.5% of the oceans is protected. One of the places earmarked for this scheme is the area around the hydrothermal vents off the Azores islands in the Atlantic Ocean.

Conservation organizations are also working with the tourist industry to make sure that divers and other visitors do not damage sensitive habitats.

Some marine parks are already well established. The Great Barrier Reef Marine Park in Australia was set up in 1975 and covers about 345,950 sq km (133,530 sq miles). The reef is also on the United Nation's list of World Heritage Sites. It is home to at least 4,000 species of mollusc, 1,500 species of fish and 400 species of coral, many of them endangered. Even so, the fragile reef system is still not safe. It remains under threat from fishing, pollution and global warming.

National parks can help preserve huge areas of coral reef from destructive activities. This is part of the Great Barrier Reef Marine Park in Australia.

Further information

International agreements

There are many agreements, treaties and organizations in place to protect the oceans and safeguard their resources and wildlife. These are just a few of them.

1. UNCLOS (United Nations Convention on the Law of the Sea) (1982)

An internationally recognized treaty dealing with all matters concerning the law of the sea. Lays down a full set of rules to protect and preserve all aspects of the marine environment, for example by preventing and reducing marine pollution. Includes rules for the safe and sustainable use of the oceans and their resources. Also promotes the efficient and peaceful use of the oceans.

2. OSPAR (Convention for the Protection of the Marine Environment of the North-East Atlantic) (1992)

A treaty signed by 14 European countries bordering the north-east Atlantic. Calls on members "to take all possible steps to prevent and eliminate pollution", and to "take the necessary measures to protect the maritime area against the adverse effects of human activities".

3. MARPOL (International Convention for the Prevention of Pollution from Ships) (1973)

Provides a full set of international guidelines for dealing with all aspects of ocean dumping and to prevent pollution from ships. It has six sections, covering oil pollution, disposal of plastics and garbage, sewage from ships and air pollution.

4. UNFA (United Nations Fisheries Agreement) (2001)

An international treaty for conserving world fisheries and protecting ocean wildlife. Aims to protect fish species, such as tuna, cod, pollock, hake and halibut, which are in danger of being overfished. Also seeks to reduce by-catch and waste in fishing and to collect detailed information on fish catches.

5. The New Common Fisheries Policy (2002)

Sets out a framework for fishing in Europe to stop overfishing and protect the marine environment. Among the main points of the agreement are:
1. Fewer new fishing boats to be built after 2004.
2. A more environmentally friendly approach to fisheries' management with recovery plans for endangered fish stocks.
3. Greater help with the scrapping of fishing boats to reduce the size of fishing fleets.

6. CITES (Convention on International Trade in Endangered Species) (1975)

Works to ban the international trade in an agreed list of endangered species, including marine animals such as sea turtles. Also monitors and regulates trade in other species that run the risk of becoming endangered.

7. UNFCCC (United Nations Framework Convention on Climate Change) (1992)

Signed by over 160 countries at the Rio Earth Summit. Recognizes that climate change affects the whole of the planet, including the oceans. Aims to reduce the levels of greenhouse gases being produced by human activities.

8. ICRAN (International Coral Reef Action Network) (2000)

A partnership of several international organizations working to stop and reverse the damage being done to the world's coral reefs. Looks at ways of monitoring and managing reefs, and at agreeing a framework for conservation. Also aims to raise people's awareness about the threats facing the reefs.

Websites

Here are a few websites to help you to find out more about the oceans:

www.whoi.edu
The website of the Woods Hole Oceanographic Institution in the USA, with information on all aspects of marine science.

www.hboi.edu
The website of the Harbor Branch Oceanographic Institution in the USA. Take a virtual trip in a Johnson Sealink II submersible to the ocean depths.

www.soc.soton.ac.uk
The Southampton Oceanography Centre in the UK with information about marine science and technology.

www.marine.csiro.au
Information about Australia's marine resources and the efforts being made to conserve them.

http://seawifs.gsfc.nasa.gov/ocean_planet.html
A virtual tour of the oceans at the Smithsonian Institution in the USA, with information about satellite monitoring.

www.panda.org
The website of the Worldwide Fund for Nature (WWF) International, with details of conservation hotspots and their latest campaigns.

www.greenpeace.org
Greenpeace's website, with details of current projects and updates on previous campaigns.

www.earthwatch.unep.net/oceans
Information about the United Nations Environment Programme which monitors the world's most endangered places, including coral reefs.

Glossary

Abyssal
Describing the part of the deep ocean that lies below about 2 km (1.2 miles).

Adapted
Having certain features or ways of behaving which allow a plant or animal to survive in a particular habitat.

Algae
A group of simple plants, ranging from tiny, one-celled plants to huge seaweeds.

Bacteria
Microscopic, single-celled living things found almost everywhere.

Benthic
Describes the seabed.

Benthos
The animals living on the seabed.

Bioluminescence
Light made by plants and animals.

Carbon dioxide
A gas found in the atmosphere. It is released when fuel, such as coal or wood, burns and when animals breathe out. It is absorbed by plants when they photosynthesize.

Condensed
When water vapour cools and turns into liquid water.

Endangered
Animals and plants that are in danger of dying out, or becoming extinct.

Epipelagic
Describing the top 100 to 150 m (330 to 490 ft) layer of the sea.

Erosion
The wearing out and shaping of the land by the weather and the sea.

Evaporate
When liquid water is heated, and turns into water vapour.

Extinction
When an animal or plant dies out forever.

Fishery
A known area for catching particular breeds of fish.

Intertidal
The part of a coast that lies between the high-tide mark and the low-tide mark.

Invertebrates
Animals that do not have backbones or skeletons inside their bodies.

Latitude
The measure of how far a place is to the north or the south of the equator.

Mesopelagic
Describing the part of the sea that lies at a depth of between 200 and 1,000 m (600 to 3,000 ft).

Nutrient
A substance in food that plants and animals need to stay alive.

Pelagic
Describing the open ocean, the water that lies above the seabed.

Photosynthesis
The process by which green plants take in sunlight, CO_2 and water to make oxygen and food.

Phytoplankton
Microscopic, single-celled plants that drift in the sea, and begin most ocean food chains.

Renewable energy
Sources of energy that can be used again and again.

Salinity
The saltiness of seawater.

Sediment
Particles of sand, gravel, clay, mud and silt that are washed into the sea from rivers and which settle on the seabed.

Sonar
Stands for Sound Navigation And Ranging. Sonar detects the position or geography of an area by sending out sounds and mapping the pattern of the returning echoes.

Storm surge
Very high sea level caused by strong winds blowing across the surface of the water.

Temperate oceans
Oceans that lie between the constantly warm tropics around the equator and the cold poles.

Vertical migration
A daily journey made by an animal up through the layers of the sea.

Water vapour
Water in the form of a gas.

Zooplankton
Tiny sea animal that grazes on phytoplankton.

Index